Sunny and friends

STORIES OF SHELTER PETS TOLD IN THEIR OWN WORDS

Janis Kell  Claudia Varjotie

WestBow Press books may be ordered through booksellers or by contacting:

WestBow Press
A Division of Thomas Nelson & Zondervan
1663 Liberty Drive
Bloomington, IN 47403
www.westbowpress.com
1 (866) 928-1240

ISBN: 978-1-5127-5180-2 (sc)
ISBN: 978-1-5127-5181-9 (e)

Library of Congress Control Number: 2016912523

Printed in the United States.

WestBow Press rev. date: 9/26/2016

WestBow
PRESS®
A DIVISION OF THOMAS NELSON
& ZONDERVAN

This book is dedicated to shelter workers everywhere and to the shelter pets they love and care for. Please adopt!

The Animal Shelter was a busy place. In the morning Melinda cleaned cages and kennels, fed and watered animals, gave medicine, walked dogs, and played with cats. Now it was time to load Sunny into the van and drive to the television studio, because lucky Sunny had been chosen to be the "Pet of the Week". Maybe this was her chance to find her purr-fect home!

Melinda and Sunny had fun at their interview. When it was finished, the news reporter told them they did a great job, and wished them good luck in finding Sunny a home. Melinda and Sunny wished for good luck, too.

That night when Melinda went to bed, she couldn't stop thinking about Sunny and all of the other wonderful animals at the shelter. Why was it that so many of them were there, and when would they finally find homes? As Melinda drifted off to sleep, she pictured herself back at the television studio, but something was very different. She was sitting in the news reporter's chair and all around her, each waiting for a turn to speak, were Sunny and many of the other shelter pets. And then… Lights! Camera! Action!

Melinda turned first to Sunny. "You are such a sweet and loving little girl," said Melinda. "How is it that you became a shelter cat?"

"Oh, I had a good life for a few years. I lived in a pretty little house with a nice lady who let me sit on her lap all day if I wanted to. I had plenty of good food to eat, toys to play with, and a wonderful warm bed. Then one day some younger people came and told my nice lady (they called her Mom) that she couldn't live alone anymore and would go to live with them. What were they talking about? She didn't live alone!

I lived with her. When they packed up her things, I thought I would be moving too, but instead they put me outside with some food and water and told me that cats can take care of themselves. When the food was gone and my belly was empty I decided to find a new home, but nobody would let me in. A family finally let me sleep on their porch for a while and the lady fed me, but she said she

couldn't keep me because I would make her son sneeze. By that time I had fleas and my fur wasn't so pretty anymore. I was getting skinny, too, so I wasn't surprised that they didn't want me. I stayed on the porch though, until one day the lady put me in a box and took me for a ride, and that's when I came to the shelter.

The nice shelter people got rid of my fleas and gave me food and a cage to sleep in. I'm very grateful, but I would really like to live in a pretty little house again and have a soft warm lap to sit on all day if I wanted to…"

Next it was Zorro's turn to tell his story.

"I once lived in a house too, but my experience was very different from Sunny's. The children thought I was a toy, and sometimes they pulled my tail and squeezed me way too tight. My fur is kind of long, but nobody ever brushed me and it got all tangled and matted. My nails were never trimmed either, and they grew so long that they curled into the pads of my feet. Boy, did that hurt! Next something went wrong inside my ears. I kept shaking my head to make the pain go away and I meowed a lot because it hurt so much.

One day when my ears were hurting more than usual, one of the children tried to pick me up. I was sure that I was going to get squeezed again, so I scratched him. I know I shouldn't have done it, but, well, I felt so

sick and I just couldn't help it. The person they called Dad said that they couldn't

have a family pet that behaved so badly, so off to the shelter I went. The shelter people were kind to me from the minute I got there. They took me to the doctor to get medicine for my ears, and then they gave me a bath, a haircut, and a nail trim. Just look at me now! I'm so handsome, I feel good, and I'm ready to find a home with people who will take good care of me!"

Melinda couldn't believe her ears as the animals took turns telling their stories. Next was Angelina.

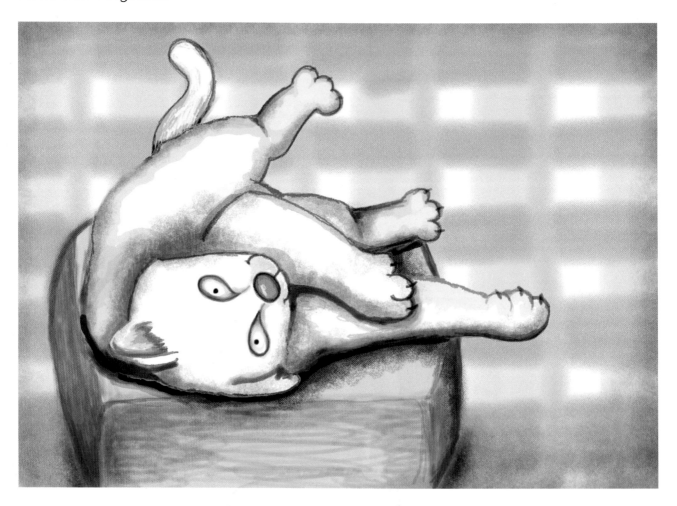

"I never had a home, at least not that I can remember. I do remember being with my mother and my brother and sister, living first in one place and then another. If the weather was bad, we would try to find shelter anywhere we could…in an empty box or a doorway or under some bushes, but most of the time we were just on the street. When we were hungry (which was pretty much always), we would jump into a garbage can to find table scraps,

or sometimes one of us would catch a mouse, or we would even steal food from someone's porch that was meant for their own pet. It was a dangerous life for a cat, with big cars whizzing by us, dogs barking and chasing us, and people yelling at us to "Scat!" One by one my mom and my siblings went their own ways, and soon

I was completely alone. One day I was *so* hungry, searching every street and alley for something to eat, when suddenly I smelled something deliciously fishy. My nose took me to a plastic box with the door wide open, and inside was a beautiful can of cat food! I went right in, and the next thing I knew the door was locked behind me. I was loaded into a van with more plastic boxes with kitties in them, and

I was on my way to the shelter. Once I got there, the people were so nice to me. They made sure I always had food and water, a bed, and even some toys, but the best thing was that they talked to me and petted me and made me feel oh so special. If that's what it's like to live in a home, I want one!"

Now Lucy, a small black cat, spoke up.

"I want you to know that I'm very nervous about being here, because I'm still afraid of most people. The house that I once lived in was not at all like Sunny's house or even Zorro's. I lived with a person who collected animals, and there were too many of us for one house. Even I knew that, but the person didn't seem to understand or care, because soon more than 30 of us were living there! It was very crowded, and since we were never allowed to go outside, the house got very dirty. If one of us got sick, we all got sick, but we never got any medicine to make us feel better. There were animals everywhere of all ages, shapes, and sizes! There wasn't much food for us to share, and sometimes there was only dog food or only cat food...we all ate the same thing. The strangest part was that the person never wanted to pet us or cuddle us, and would even give us a kick when we rubbed against his legs. I couldn't understand why he wanted us if he didn't want to love us, and I made up my mind that people were not to be trusted. One

day some people wearing uniforms came into the house and told our person that his animals were being taken away from him. We were all loaded into a big truck that took us to the shelter. Some of my friends found homes quickly, but I couldn't forget my bad experiences and I guess I didn't behave very well. The shelter people were worried about me, but then one of the shelter ladies took me home and gave me extra special attention. So now I am in foster care, but from the way she hugs me and cuddles me, I have a feeling that I've found my forever home!"

Melinda then turned to Jupiter, who was being very quiet, and said, "Jupiter, what

a big boy you are, but you look so sad. Let's hear a dog's story about how you came to the shelter."

"Yes, I *am* big as most Great Danes are, and that is part of the reason I came to the shelter. When I was just a few weeks old, a family adopted me. There was a

mom and a dad and four children who loved me very much and tried their best to take good care of me. The house we lived in was sort of small, but there was a little yard that the children and I could play in. It was wonderful at the beginning, but I was a growing boy and boy did I grow!

Soon the house and the yard seemed much smaller. Every time I turned around it seemed that I was knocking something or someone over. When we went out to play, I could only run a few steps before my nose would hit the fence. I also heard the people talking about how much food I ate. Don't get me wrong. They fed me every day and it was good, healthy food, but there just wasn't enough of it. I guess with four children to feed, there wasn't always enough money left to feed me, too. One day everyone seemed sad, and they didn't want to look at me. The adults were talking very quietly, and then the children started to cry. That's when the dad said that we would go for a ride, and he took me to the shelter. When he said goodbye I was so confused. . .they loved me, so why was I here? The shelter people were very nice to me, and now I understand that they will find a home for me with a house and a yard and a supper dish that will be big enough for a big dog like me. I can't wait!"

The next to speak were two little dachshunds, Heckel and Jeckel, who shared a chair.

"Our home before the shelter was a place where people came to buy puppies, so we had lots of brothers and sisters and our mom was always having more. We couldn't wait to be adopted, but we didn't understand why no one ever chose us.

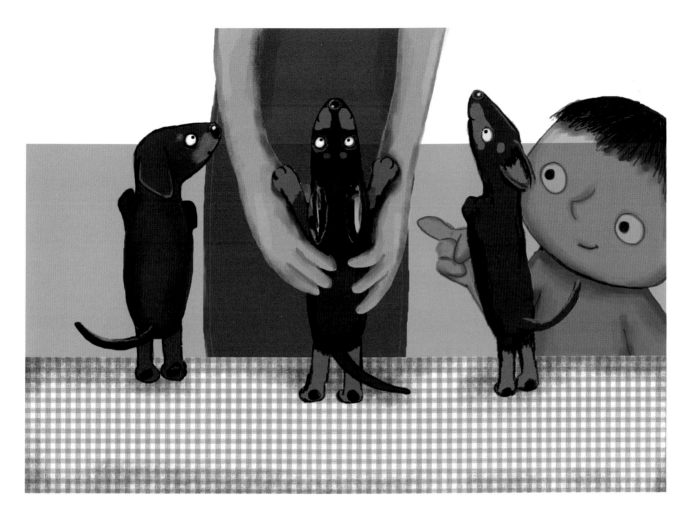

Then we heard someone say that we had 'special needs.' It seems that our front legs didn't grow right before we were born, so we both have little stubs where our front legs should be. We were never worried though, because we were able to play and snuggle and do many things that our brothers and sisters could do. But as the weeks went by, we started to realize that 'special needs' must mean that nobody would ever want us. How sad we were! One day the people who owned us said that since we couldn't be sold, we would have to be surrendered and that's when we came to the shelter. We didn't know what to expect and we were scared, but the shelter people were so kind to us. They contacted a group called a 'Dachshund Rescue' where dachshunds with special needs get extra special care until they can be matched with a family who doesn't mind that their new pet is older, or needs a lot of medicine or an operation, or has front legs that don't look and work like they should. We'll soon be moving to the 'Dachshund Rescue'... one step closer to our forever homes!"

As soon as Heckel and Jeckel finished, Jove began to speak.

"I have special needs, too, but you can't tell by looking at me. The shelter people tell me that I'm a beautiful and very friendly cat, but I have what's called feline immunodeficiency virus (FIV). I never had a real home, but I lived in a neighborhood where everyone was nice to me, petted me, and many people left food and water for me outside so I never really had to worry about having enough to eat. In the wintertime someone would let me sleep in their garage, or in a nice box they would fix for me with a roof on it and warm blankets inside. Life was pretty good, until one day a big old tomcat, a stranger in town, came into my territory. He growled, I hissed, and the next thing I knew the fur was flying. I chased him away, but I had scratches all over and a deep bite on my neck that was bleeding a lot. I didn't feel so good after my fight, so one of the people who fed me took me to the doctor.

The doctor fixed me up, and also gave me some shots and tested me for FIV, which came back positive. Since the people didn't know much about FIV or how to care for me, they decided to take me to the shelter. That's where I learned that even though I can't live outdoors anymore, I'll be able to have a happy and normal life if someone is willing to give me an indoor home. It's fine for me to live with people and also dogs, because they can't catch FIV. I can even have kitty-siblings if they are FIV-positive like me. Just make sure I get regular check-ups and routine shots, and I can be around to love you for a long time!"

Last but not least, it was Eden's turn to tell her story.

"I was always the type of dog to be adventurous, running after squirrels, chasing any unusual smell that reached my nose, and making friends with everyone I met. Even though I had a nice big fenced yard to play in, I wanted to see the world. It was easy for me to unlatch the gate…it was broken and no one ever fixed it. I had gotten out a few times before, but someone always caught me and put me back in the yard. I decided one day that if I got out again I would run like the wind, and I did! Nobody saw me leave, and I was free! I ran until I was out of breath, then I rested a while and ran some more. Along the way I found some children to play with, and one of them decided to take me home with him. When I got

there, the big people in the family said that I must belong to someone because I was well-cared for and clean, but I wasn't wearing any collar or tag that said where I lived or who I belonged to. They didn't know what to do with me, so they put me in the car and took me to a different house. All at once I realized that I had no idea where I was, but being adventurous, I was ready to go anywhere with anyone. As the weeks went by I lived in three different houses. Everyone was nice to me and said that I must belong somewhere, but nobody knew where. Finally someone brought me to the shelter, to see if *they* could find my real owner. The shelter people checked me for a microchip (that's a tiny thing under my skin with my owner's information on it), but there was none. No one had called looking for me, and there was nothing in the newspaper under 'Lost and Found.' Since no one could find my owner, I'm up for adoption now. It's not bad living here, but I really hope I get to live in a house with a yard again soon."

Suddenly, Melinda's alarm clock rang. It was time to get up and go to work, but what a dream she'd had! Later that morning as she went about her shelter chores, she came to Sunny's cage. "How's my sweet little kitty today?" Melinda asked as she reached into the cage. As she took Sunny out and looked into her furry little face, she was sure that Sunny winked at her!

These stories are based on actual animals who have lived at the Hancock County, WV Animal Shelter. Some have been adopted and some are still waiting to find their forever homes. Proceeds from this book will be donated for the benefit of shelter pets.